EVERYDAY
PRAYERS
for

Grandmothers

Margaret Anne Huffman

DIMENSIONS
FOR LIVING

NASHVILLE

EVERYDAY PRAYERS FOR GRANDMOTHERS

94 95 96 97 98 99 00 01 02 03—10 9 8 7 6 5 4 3 2 1

This book is printed on acid-free recycled paper.

ISBN 0-687-12179-5

For
Gary
". . . this is my beloved and my friend,"
Song of Solomon 5:16*b*
Lynn, Rob, Beth, the enrichment
and
. . . for **Aaron** and **Kali,** to begin with

MANUFACTURED IN THE UNITED STATES OF AMERICA

Contents

Down on My Knees—
Introduction

I'm down on my knees, Lord, and can't get up.

My tennis knee has locked, and my back's kinked into an everlasting slouch as I pick up dolly shoes, mini-trucks, wheels, books, cereal circles, and snippets of yarn from finger crocheting left in the wake of the grandchildren's visit. A faint dusting of flour is sifted with contented abandon over it all in satisfied benediction from our afternoon of baking homemade doggy biscuits.

I find you down here, too, Lord, at the height where I have my best moments with these wondrous small people, my grandchildren. You and they both are best approached from my knees where, eye to eye, we can greet one another across the events of the days we share.

Goodbye, Granny

Where, Lord, have the grandmothers
gone? The ones who pulled down green
window shades against late afternoon sun,
who knew how to make hollyhock dollies
and snapdragon puppets? Who were always
home, usually in the kitchen or garden?
Who concocted soothing elixirs when we
were sick? Who hooked up our summers to
sprinklers, before days of plastic sliders,
pre-fab summer fun?

Where, Lord, have the grandmothers
gone?

We've gone to offices, hospitals, court-
houses, laboratories, factories, board rooms
and back to school. We've gone to condo-
miniums, apartments, and energy-efficient
and technology-bright homes.

I'd love to tend my grandbaby this week,
concocting elixirs and potions, if I could,
Lord, while she and her mommy are ill with

bronchitis. But she lives a long train ride away and I have a time clock to punch.

It's a perplexing, unexpected discovery, Lord, like hitting a speed bump a little too fast on the highway, and I've recently been feeling the jolts.

Grandmothering has gone the way of the hand-cranked ice cream freezer, Lord, and I've left myself behind, I'm discovering, and I can't keep up with this younger generation's scattering either! I am lonely for a full house, for a steamed-up-window kitchen, for conversation closer than airmail stamps and long-distance phone calls connecting me to both ancestors and descendants.

I want to be an old-fashioned granny, Lord, like I used to have, for this is not enough.

And so did you enjoy our detour last week, past a toy store? It was from your inspiration that I bought two matching tiny tea sets, old-fashioned roses twining their way around the delicate cups and pot, one to keep, one to mail to my grand-daughter. Ever so often, we will "get together," by telephone for a brief tea party served from our companion sets.

It's difficult to feel separated over sips of fresh-brewed love.

Where have all the grannies gone, Lord? We're right here, caught up in new lives that are so different from our grandmothers' that we are faint erasures of those old days, old ways.

Yet help us, though, to value who we are today with our mobility, options and contributions. *New-fashioned* will become *old-fashioned* soon enough, Lord, for each generation is on its own cutting edge, and today is as good as yesterday was for our grandmothers.

Where have all the grannies gone? Hither and yon, here and there, at home and gone, Lord, but never too far away from your re-creating love. Help us, through it, to find togetherness times with our grandchildren, great-grandchildren, Lord, even if held at long-distance.

Box Houses

She's perfectly at home, Lord, having claimed the dishwasher carton the minute the plumber discarded it. Do you see her through the windows and a door I cut out? She colored them silver. An oatmeal box makes a tip-tilted but serviceable chimney; shoe boxes, window flower gardens.

In went dolls, books, blanket and toy tractor. She's secured it all with a ring of old keys, putting them carefully in the bottom of her dress-up purse each time she leaves home.

"I want to eat lunch in here, Mammaw."

After a moment's hesitation—after all, aren't we supposed to eat at tables?—I relented, changing my menu to accomodate her new home's dining facilities.

So few things are from a child's-eye viewpoint, for they are outnumbered, overshadowed and dwarfed by the gigantic trappings of our adult world.

In a cardboard home, in a fairy-tale forest, in a land beyond, she has taken up residence for these first times away from home. A safe first move, she in the middle of her own living room with a baby-sitting Mammaw in the kitchen, as far away as she needs me to be.

Sometimes I go for tea, even though only part of me fits in her cozy home. "You can eat on my porch, Mammaw," invites a child already leading us toward letting her go places none of us may follow. A mother's tale, a grandmother's tale, for, Lord, do you also recall those tent-house lunches we shared with her mother, her aunt and uncle not so long ago?

Thank you, Lord, for nests. From those first rich tapestries woven from our womanly flesh to the imaginative ones these busy grandchildren fashion from boxes and sofa cushions. Curl up with them and enjoy the coziness of children come home to a space that fits them as snugly as the palm of your hand.

Making Sense of It

Flowers smell, this we know, Lord, for which we give you thanks. And, in your infinite wisdom, you created woods which also smell. Walnut especially. And oak. And pine, with Christmas in its pores.

I'd forgotten to smell, Lord, until, bending down in obedience to my granddaughter's insistence, I discovered that grass has a fragrance, too. Grinning in snaggletoothed delight at *my* delight in the aroma of turf, she, as if hand-in-hand with you, toddled off to sniff out other ordinary delights to share with me.

Children roll on, sniff, rub, scoot, taste, and touch things we bypass, if not actually disdain or ignore, we confess Creator Lord.

Meanwhile, our skin, like our spirits and minds, gets calluses on it. Our eyes glaze; our ears plug out important noises, Lord, composer of it all, like clocks ticking, crickets serenading, leaves falling, water dripping.

They are, however, music to a child's ears, magical feasts for their eyes and hands concocted from a daily world we are invited to visit again as their guests, renewing as we do our pleasure in your sensory world.

Why not try it, you suggest? Sniff a tree. Or an old gold necklace. Rub a stone, lick a lemon. Listen to ice melt in a glass.

May we accept your invitation, Lord, for we are out of touch, as the saying goes. Also out of sight, out of hearing distance, too, into the breadth of your world. Thank you for the fresh awareness that can be ours if we but crawl along in the wake of a delighted grandchild.

Love's Language

We needed a translator today, didn't we, Lord, as my husband and I drawled in unison, *"HAHHHH, HAHHH, HAHHH,"* at a rather bemused waiter serving us sizzling kebobs. *"Hot, Hot, Hot,"* is another way of saying it, but the grandbaby has taught us better words.

She is teaching the family *her* language, *her* labels and value system as we echo *her* first words, not vice versa, Lord, and I am an apt pupil.

We have, following your lead, O, Lord, who applauds, not corrects, all our efforts, opted for communicating rather than correcting her: **"No,** HOT, *not HAHHH.* **No,** *that's not a 'Doot,' it's a duck, dog, doll."* This is her interchangeable exclamation of recognition and love for stuffed animals and people, so a *'Doot'* she calls it, and a *'Doot'* it is until **she,** Lord, is ready to associate our other labels.

14

And as her daddy pointed out when she was lavishing love on her favorite "Doot of the Day" with the same intensity as on us, "We are, to her, just big 'Doots.'" A label, Lord, I wear proudly even while eating my "*HAHHH, HAHHH, HAHHH*" lunch.

Why start when they are less tall than our pockets to correct, compete, control, capture and re-create them in battles over whose truth to live by, whose word to speak? You don't treat us this way, Lord, so why should we do it to these small others?

And multiply these toddler skirmishes, Lord, for sixteen years: can you imagine the wrangles over car keys, curfews? Any time you have to become a general with small children, my grandmother reminded me when I was a new mother, you have already lost. Not the battle, of course, for big people have always been able to force small people to do their bidding, but the point of the journey: companionship spoken in a shared vocabulary of love. Thank you for giving us examples and a glossary of love words to use.

Cake Crumbs

They are moving away, Lord, taking a ball-throwing, laugh-making grandson a train, plane-ride away. His last night's birthday party was a farewell, too, Lord, and cake crumbs write a forlorn postscript to its fun. Before me, too, are footprints made in the shaggy carpet, of the dance he led us in, spinning, leaping high in the air, to joyful traveling music. I cannot vacuum up these footprints, Lord, for it will erase every trace of our dance.

A keeper of old things, I collect antiques, memories, logs for my home's wall, and I rebuff change whenever possible. Yet, I crave adventure and would be the first grandmother in outer space if there were a rocket seat available. Two squabbling parts of me, Lord, that at transitions like this, threaten to pull me apart!

As everyone has grown up and gone

away, I am the one who feels uprooted, as if I were the one leaving, but I have no boxes to pack, no new home to decorate. And I worry: can I find my way to some place new? Am I becoming a rut-loving old woman? Am I stuck?

I need reassurance. Actually I want guarantees, I confess, Lord, that everything will be okay, that I can find my way in something new. I can sometimes feel your presence, Lord of dusty feet and sojourners, as a tickle of curiosity about the future becomes as beckoning and lovely as my freshly smooth carpet waiting for my foot-prints going in new directions, following where others invite; to dance new dances.

Be with me as I help them pack; as I memorize new addresses; help me smile, waving them on, in their rearview mirror on that moving day.

Hum the first notes of a new song in my ear, Lord, so that I may enjoy the steps of this new dance with Change, the partner you have sent to lead me forward.

Name Calling

I held you close beside me today, Lord,
at the Memorial Day picnic where I ate
three chicken legs fried from my namesake
Mammaw's famous recipe and counted relatives . . . begat, begat, begat.

Cause or effect: which has Mammaw's
faith been for me? Even at a half century of
life, I have no clear answer, Lord. Nonethe-
less, I'm sharing "my" verse with our
granddaughter, repeating it as I name her
in daily prayer for your hearing, your
enjoyment, your companionable caring.

Remember how I marveled, "*I* have a
verse?" when I discovered Mammaw's
marked-up Bible long before I could read? I
only knew we weren't supposed to write in
books and was fascinated by this discrep-
ancy in a grandmother who always minded
the rules.

And, Lord, there it was: Romans 8:28
". . . all things work together for good . . ."

with a firmly written *"Margaret Anne"* in the margin.

Sometimes I've easily believed all things DO work together despite circumstances to the contrary; sometimes I have not, I confess Lord. Always, though, I have believed that Mammaw believed, her faith in you connecting me to others who believed and were sustained, enriched, by that believing.

She believed enough to daily call my name to you and recite my verse—along with everyone else's in the family—as if she also believed I could find its promised strength. And, Lord, anyone with such a fine inheritance as a name-calling belief feels rich, feels valued, feels known.

Cause and effect: which has she been?

Perhaps we will find out, as the verse, like relatives' addresses and secret fried chicken recipes, gets handed on. Lord, be with this child through all things as you are for me, a grandmother at my side.

Tom Thumb

Meet Tom Thumb, Lord, the tiniest little boy imagination could create. Yet he's not imaginary, he's a real little boy, a friend's grandbaby, complete with all his parts. They work in microscopic efficiency when aided by machines that dwarf a body measured in ounces and centimeters.

Will he ever throw a rubber ball on a day burning gently in fall beauty? Will he laugh, talk back and forget to do his homework? Will he collect frogs, bugs and, in time, girls' phone numbers? His chances are good in this place where figuring the odds is about all there is for such little ones. That and relying on your Spirit which often defies the odds.

Too weak even to cry now, Lord, he is growing up only in the fervent dreams and prayers of his parents and grandparents, noses pressed to the special nursery glass.

In their stroking fingers that must substitute for holding and rocking him. In the nurses' lullabies when he seems fretful as if to wonder where he is so suddenly too soon.

You can hold them, Lord, for your touch is oh, so gentle with these little ones who've burst into life not quite ready for them. Breathe into his nostrils that are but dots on his face; soothe his tissue-paper skin with your comfort so that he will not waste energy dodging pain. Swaddle him in the assurance that you are nearby, ready to answer him even though he is too weak to cry out for you.

Strengthen the parents; give the mother milk overflowing to be fed birdlike into his hungry mouth; give the father patience and a tenderness he'd never thought to need. Guide them toward each other, Lord, and together toward you, the God of growing boys.

Fixing Cakes

No birthday songs to sing, Lord, no presents to wrap, no cards to sign . . . the birthday boy, seventeen, will attend today's family gathering in spirit only. "I always made his cakes," his grandmother cried in grief so intense that I felt its hot breath.

O Lord, can there be grief greater? A child's death is incomprehensible and impossible to prepare for; it is the most unnatural.

Bless those, Lord, who meet in worldwide clusters of understanding. A club no one wants to join, its membership dues are high: death of a child, Lord, an unbearable price to pay, especially alone; sit among them.

And so, often, Lord, you are the only one who hears a dead child's, grandchild's name spoken aloud, for to many of us, it's "out of sight, out of mind." Forgive our short memories and insensitive forgetfulness.

So thank you, God of comfort, for such groups as this, where grief can be what it truly is, an action verb. Bless these fellow sufferers who listen when the rest of us, embarrassed and uneasy, turn away from parental tears, recalled events, names spoken. Visit each one around the table with the will to grieve, the determination to go on; assure them that they can go on, Lord, without abandoning their child to the past.

Inspire and equip others outside this terrible membership to speak their names, send cards on birth and death anniversaries; to not turn away at tears or memories. Make us bigger and stronger, Lord, for ours is the easiest burden: we only have to be embarrassed and a little uncomfortable.

Be with me as I invite this grandmother with idled hands into my kitchen to make a memory cake for her grandchild gone, but not forgotten; we will write his name in sprawling, bright frosting letters like the love messages he wrote indelibly on his grandma's heart.

Blankies, Lambies, and Thumbs

Nights are getting warmer as May days lengthen, Lord; time to replace my flannel sheets. Time to remake my nest.

For it, I require a soaking-bath prelude to a fat pillow, quilt, book and reading light tilted just so; prayers come with lights off, Lord, where I find you at the edge of rest. We find comfort where we can, in rituals, tokens, talismans, for, as you know, Lord, we are just little folks in big skins.

Next door, gently snoring, is a little lady clutching a paper dinosaur, a shred of her mother's bathrobe and a blanket her brother sometimes uses; downstairs, he sleeps with nightlight burning, nearby, a toy raccoon.

Why, then, gentle Lord, do we prematurely separate these young ones from their comfortings by painting thumbs bitter? By burning Blankies or Lambies before their frantic eyes? By shaming their needs?

A grown-up son, bringing it out to show me last summer—remember, Lord?—unashamedly nuzzled old Lambie when he came upon him while cleaning his room in preparation for a major cross-country move. How would he be braver, Lord, more adventurous, if I'd tossed Lambie far beyond his reach?

For when they are twenty-five years old, Lord, and rediscover Lambie nestled among yellowing baby clothes and first drawings in a trunk, our children, grandchildren, will remember **not** how hard it was to give up or guilt for needing it, but rather the comfort they knew, the assumptions it taught. Easy lessons to translate into reliance upon your ever-present security.

Let us pause at the knees of these wise grandchildren, Lord, for we misunderstand security, needlessly withholding ourselves from the grace-full warmth of your robe, the grasp of your hand. Snuggle us a little, Lord.

Swingin' on the Garden Gate

Mondays are tennis; Tuesdays, book club; Wednesdays, cooking class; Thursdays, art lessons. Fridays, free. A schedule for us grownups, Lord? Nope, a five-year-old I know, granddaughter of a friend who, she laments, practically has to make an appointment to see the child. And then they have to *Go Do Something Important* or it is a wasted day. But can any of your days be wasted, Lord?

But our grandkids are mini-CEOs, in charge of their enterprises, Lord, following tight schedules, moving from one demand to another and spending how many hours a day in the car?

Come to Grandma's and swing on the garden gate, I want to invite, checking to see if I still have one, for I, too, I confess, Lord, haven't swung on it in awhile. Have we grandmas set our feet on too fast a track?

Yet garden gates have become suspect, for when we see a child swinging on one, we quickly think up another activity to "enrich" their days. Or we scold them, "Go find something to do!"

They have. Instead of the nothing we assume, they are involved in one of their best, most important tasks: play. How can we have forgotten, Lord, our own delicious carefree childhoods when, left to our own devices, we simply played. Indoors or out, rain or shine, rich or poor, we played on those proverbial and literal garden gates.

Time is so compressed we adults are always behind, racing to catch up with moments we've already squandered by being so hurried. The children can't keep up with the pace we've set them.

Slow at least us grandparents down long enough to catch up with them, bringing them home to Grandma's to swing on a garden gate, for it is you gently pushing us back and forth, back and forth, simply enjoying the ride.

Second Time Around

A lizard eyed the wedding punch bowl
the day I became a grandmother. Dressed in
its finest bright blue long-tailed suit, Lord,
how had it known that color was the bride's
favorite? The shade of a small boy's eyes?

He is noticeably absent from many
casual photos of that days wedding of his
father to our daughter, tending as he was
to his lizard. That critter was a welcome
diversion, Lord, for which I thank you, on
a perplexing day for a child, officially now
a stepchild. And a stepgrandchild, lost
between what was once, would never be
again, and was not yet. It was, too, a dove,
for a new stepgrandmother who wondered
how to love this child who could only
mourn the events tying us, like so many
wedding gift bows, together.

I'd scooted over to make room for you,
too, the night before, Lord, as the child

and I sat on the stairs in quiet conversation about the bittersweet event he was torn between celebrating and mourning. For, Lord of Alpha and Omega, to welcome the new is to forever accept the departure of the old.

And he was lost, Lord, between them.

Until you and he found the critter beneath the sidewalk: a bright blue lizard, soon to be draped gently and proudly across his hand and returning my stare over the punch bowl as he introduced us.

Thank you, Lord, for it amazingly survived a full day of loving . . . much as the child did, too. I spied the lizard the other day, and, like this new grandmother, it waits for a small boy's return.

For there are, O Lord of small boys and blue lizards and ready-made grandmothers, adventures to share.

Birthday Bath

The grandfather clock has long ago chimed its pumpkin hour of midnight, Lord, and the grandfather himself is dozing on the couch, too tired to find the bed; let's leave him there for a few minutes longer, Lord, for he's worked hard today blowing up balloons, playing "Where's Bappaw?"

A first birthday party is now memory to be replayed on the VCR, and, Lord of Celebrations, all I want is a soaking bath as benediction to it.

Rubber Ducky, though, has beaten me to it, floating happily across the baby's soap-scummy, forgotten bath water. Let me rest a few minutes as the water slowly runs out, just like my sluggish energy.

Time, however, is running at a different speed, for where has the past year gone— all the now-adult's childhoods leading up to tonight, Lord?

What price am I willing to pay for a clean bathtub? For no towels on the floor? For a sensible bedtime in these my middle years? What price to have never known this little girl who is naming me "Mummmmmmaw"?

I hear your echoing, agreeing silence, Lord: none.

As I refill the tub with chamomile bubbles, I can feel my soul, like the bathtub, sink, garbage, dryer and refrigerator, overflowing with the joyous clutter of family. Thank you for the reminder, your hand on my shoulder as I rest my head against the tub in reverent gratitude.

In the serendipitous tradition of loaves and fishes picnics, Mary and Martha dinners, water into wine parties, and alabaster jar sharings, may I never let wearying dailiness, even the desire for a clean bathtub, prevent the ordinary from becoming the extraordinary it was intended to be; can be upon the acceptance of the your re-creating invitation to make all things new. Even leftover bathwater.

Dandelions

She brought me a bouquet of dandelions, Lord, a gathering of your spring sunshine that, in a grandchild's hands, transform weeds into flowers more priceless than roses.

And, Lord of hopeful solutions, in the hands of our grandchildren, dandelions might well also become the status symbol of the eco-correct nineties. They give testimony to yards where birds can feast, bees sip, dogs roam, and children roll without fear of poison. Not bad for the future generations we worry about in these days of disappearing air, water, and creatures; prod us into paying attention to these young ecologists.

Yet the dandelions of their youth grow where pesticides are spread by workers in goggles and boots who leave behind skull-and-cross-bones flags as proof of a job well done. And so, Lord who mourns with us at the sight, neither animal, vegetable nor laughing grandchild is safe from our diligent eradication of sworn enemies: dandelions in our yards.

Forgive us, Lord, for they are a metaphor for an environmental arrogance that deprives us of dandelion salads and our grandchildren of magical floating seeds to carry their giggles aloft into the fear-free ozone. We confess that we are not good stewards, Lord, who gives us both dandelions and grandchildren to grace our springs.

Bless dandelions and givers of them, Lord. And if we must be undandelioned to keep up with the neighbors, put a hoe in our hands and hope in our hearts, for we are poisoning ourselves with worry as thoroughly as our lawns with potions.

Hope and hoes, not bad tools to pass on, generation to generation.

Soft Spots

It was like a page from that first scene in creation, Lord, complete with apples and fruitful knowledge as the old-fashioned apple peeler coiled red ribbons onto the floor. Patiently, the toddler, here to visit Mammaw and Bappaw, sang to herself while she watched and waited for the apple we were dividing for a mid-morning snack.

Half and half, the apple was brownish and softening on one side, fine on the other. Handing the perfect slices to her, Lord, without questioning, I ate the soft, browning ones myself.

There was no question, Lord, about which half I would take, for I am— although grandmother now—always a mother. And, in your nurturing footsteps, Lord, mothers always take soft spots in apples, back seats in cars, and heels of bread.

Why apologize? Why protest? We are called by you, Lord, to the glory of being second, a position from which to sing a "Magnificat" of daily life. Like Mary we understand that to be second is not to be less. It is, Lord, to be chosen for a role no one else can fill, that of providing the means for creation.

And in that drama, there are no second string players, no bit parts.

But, Lord, we don't fully understand this business of being handmaidens, of being second, of stepping back and standing down so that our children and grandchildren can move ahead. Help us to see that we and our brown-spotted apples are the means to your ends.

Thanks to your grace, second place is never second-rate.

A Stitch in Time

Do you know who she is, Lord? This funny lady returning my gaze in the mirror? She wears red-rimmed bifocals and has smile lines written indelibly around her mouth by wry, amusing thoughts. A few steel-wool gray hairs, like hash-marks on a tablet, keep a tally of her days.

Who is she? Since today's announcement from a long-distance daughter, she is that most amazed of creatures, a fledgling grandmother.

Who would've thought, Lord, in all this middle-year familiar routine and well-worn responses, that such an eruption of joy, awe, and downright giddy excitement could burn in my withering bosom?

A grandchild. A miracle being knit by you beneath the heart of us all; beneath a grandmother's hand as I answer the infant's kicks with a caressing promise of rocking chair lullabies, of high-swing-flying days.

My hands need to be busy, Lord, in these days of preparation, so I am making a comforter for whom I secretly believe will be my granddaughter.

I am stitching into its squares, Lord, the hopes and commitments for your peaceful world begun in that mothering decade; making it soft with stuffings of your promised companionship I found then. Tying it at each corner with ribbons of your grace which sustains me still, I am knotting each with a certain tug that only a grandmother can give, a satisfying, secure and double-knotted bow of joy.

Like stray buttons and snippets of thread settled in the bottom of my sewing basket are the memories from those long ago days of my babies, Lord, which I've kept in my heart and pondered. They've been saved in the treasure box of memory-hope until now, until the day, Lord, we began stitching a grandmother's love.

Stepping Stones

There is a fish in our river, Lord, who leads a charmed life. We heard it the other night—splat!—as it jumped from the water.

As surely as little minnows swim in its coolness, the river was your gift that long ago day; the fish, your blessing sign as I met my stepgrandson over the span of pole and line.

There is more than one way to get grandchildren, Lord of limitless possibilities, and many of us are privileged to learn to live "in step" with second-family children. And in the doing, it takes time to build a past, to construct assumptions, memories, and security.

For us, it began with a fish.

An ordinary bass caught and landed by this small boy, it lived for awhile upside down in a paper cup. Then, second chances all around that day, Lord, it was set free by one who also knew how it felt to be caught . . . caught in the weeds of change.

I don't know how long fish live, Lord, but this one is sure to last as long as it's needed, splashing, jumping clear of the water, nudging the shallows in reminder of the blessings of a late summer day and loving families that last.

You never doubted, did you Lord, that we'd understand the message of your fish, symbol of your recreating power? As it swam away, it carried on rainbow gills our worries, doubts and tensions. Like us, it revels in the free-flowing stream of new life and fresh days; like us, too, it bears the marks of the hooks of disruption and pain; and also like us, it thanks you for a small blond boy with a smiling heart and kind hands. No matter that we'd not known him before; today, he is a part of our family, like the legend we retell over and over of "The Fish That Got Away."

Tell Me a Story, Sing Me a Song

As soon as I met him, Lord, I wrote a story, a sonnet of joy for his life. He is my stepgrandson, a tow-headed adventurer who turned my life upside down in a cart-wheel of wondrous change.

He crowned me a grandmother with his gentle pats on my head; he opened doors to me with his inquiring mind and inviting hand, Lord, this special grandson who came ready-made at the hand of his Dad.

And now he has a baby sister, making me grandmother again.

As soon as I met this tiny lady-child, I broke into song, Lord, an ode of joy for her life.

Yes, Lord, for my life, too, for I am enjoying being a grandmother because of what I finally learned in all the mothering years: putting away toys is not worth battles; taking naps together helps; it is not possible to snuggle too much; save all the crayon drawings and three-word "stories;" write in baby books and on backs of pictures.

This is an easy time, Lord, one of reaping and savoring.

Bless all our life stages, Lord, flowing like seasons one into another in seamless days of creativity, strength, worry, tiredness, joy. Thank you for the chance to blend ourselves into many-lined sonnets and medleys about our children and grandchildren.

Help us listen to all our selves, Lord, old, young, new, experienced, for we grandmothers will be forever learning joyful new verses.

Cheerleaders

She was the most homely twelve-year-old, Lord, I'd seen in a long time. An ugly duckling in braces, eyeglasses, and long-legged awkwardness whose sisters are already swans. Her efforts at trying to be invisible beneath parental dismay and sisterly scorn, Lord, are painful to watch.

She, however, is the most beautiful twelve-year-old her grandmother sees, Lord, and I offer a prayer of gratitude for the grandmother's vision. It is a bridge for the "duckling" to cross on her way to better days and prettier reflections in the mirror of straight teeth, contact lenses, willowy posture; of generous, loving self-esteem.

I offer a prayer of gratitude for my grandmother who saw beyond my homemade haircuts, shin-scraped, elbow-bruised body and giggly foolishness to who I am now. It never occurred to me, Lord, that it might not happen, for her cheers were always in my ears, often drowning out my own doubts and dreadful adolescent introspection and others' frustrations.

And now I am among those women, Lord, sitting as one in the Grandmother Cheering Section.

We sit in the corners of their lives, Lord, the awkward, ungainly and sometimes unwashed—literally, if they are teens—and cheer loudly and happily, for we grandmothers can see beyond the surface into the essence of these children who may be the despair of others. They can count on us to hold up different mirrors than others do, Lord, into the awesome possibilities of who they can become. Help us hold the mirror steady.

To Diaper or Not to Diaper

I've taped myself to the grandbaby's newfangled disposable diaper more than once, Lord, as I learn about grandmothering in a world where even changing babies is controversial.

All the evidence is not yet in, but for now no one knows whether cloth or paper diapers are most environmentally catastrophic. We have many such muddles, Lord, making mountains of garbage that reach halfway to your heavens.

Diapers: what a debate to inherit, I thought yesterday as I changed the innocent, wee bottom in question.

And what about those message infant "Onesies" for grandbabies, Lord, with pictures of vanishing forests, harp seals, wolves and whales, some of the most wonderful creatures you lent us. We have already enlisted these little folk in the efforts, Lord, and even as I applaud the visual reminder—

a mandate—for all who see and smile at these precious babies, I worry they will feel burdened by the task they already carry on their backsides. I know how I feel, Lord, as I look at the shirt I am wearing today and read upside-down pleas to care about wetlands, and to care now.

I do care, Lord, for I live beside a wooded wetland and revel in pileated woodpecker families, trilium, beaver, blue herons, and the loons visiting just last night. I want my grandchildren to know the raccoon who visits us nightly; the woodchuck and her roly-poly babies; to hear the warbler's summons to morning.

As generations joined in a message T-shirt brigade, Lord, help us revere Mother Earth as you intended. Guide us as we struggle with issues that cling like so much diaper sticky tape, especially the one of despair; use your re-creating power to recycle it into determined change. Along the way, Lord, keep us old folks supplied with the energy to pick up this land-and-sea covered ball we dropped.

Old Counterpane of Love

"Mammaw kiss Bappaw," the grandchild squeals in delight. She knows a good thing when she sees it, Lord, for one of the best parts of being a grandmother is sharing the adventure . . . and life . . . with a grandfather.

I am fortunate, Lord, and not a day of what is sometimes pretty predictable routine between long-time partners goes by without my prayers of gratitude. And a hug around his grandfatherly neck.

I like to think we are inspiration, Lord, a massive oak tree for our children and grandchildren as we stand and sway under the gales of modern life. If we can do it, Lord, anyone can build a marriage to last long enough to reap grandchildren.

Children, Lord, even the adult variety, often overlook the pleasure in a middle-age or elderly marriage; they think they invented love. Yet grandchildren have no problem casting grandparents in romantic adventures, seeing beyond the gray and wrinkles to the souls of playmates.

Remind us to look through these grandchildren's sparkling eyes at one another, past the inevitable signposts of aging. These are days, Lord, when we can become mellow and rich in love, glowing with the patina of fine, vintage furniture lovingly tended by our clasped, calloused hands.

Keep us together; the grandchildren are playing on our roots.

Divorce Reroutes

She's keeping her grandchildren today, Lord, while her daughter and son-in-law are in divorce court.

Who knows when . . . if . . . the grandchildren will be back. There's no question, though, that innocence won't.

In the shrillness of a single phone call, loyalties switch, Lord, and beloved grandchildren become endangered creatures snared in the trap of divorce.

What a world, Lord. I cringe at the sight of us drawing up sides in wars over weekends, holidays, going to see Grandma. For most, divorce is not an easy decision, Lord. Be at the mediation table with them so it does not get any worse. Be with the families where violence, abuse, misuse and cruelty cannot be healed except by amputation; shield and heal the little children in the shelter of your grandmotherly arms.

And at the same time, Lord, restrain all adults from retaliation via the kids. Especially press your shushing hand over the mouths of grandmothers who would poison young minds with gossip, interrogations, and accusations against once-loved children-in-law. The kids must, with the wisdom of Solomon, Lord, cope with both halves of their lives. Let the grandmothers fortunate enough to still have visiting grandkids help by example. Give them words with which to support the children's attempts even when they disagree; help them keep their distance.

Above all, Lord, give both these oldest and youngest the assurance of your presence. In time may they seek one another to heal distances made by others' shortsighted decisions to keep them apart whether through divorce or, as can also happen, just ordinary selfishness.

And in the nighttime, Lord, when toys in the corner cast a faint shadow on the wall, comfort the grandmothers who suddenly have no one to play with.

Fellow Travelers

Nursing home visiting day. With little more than a curious, smiling glance at Great-Mammaw's nursing home mates, Lord, my trio of children arranged chairs in a circle around the piano. As if escorting royalty, Lord, I watched that long ago day as they wheeled their great-grandmother to her place of honor at the piano. There, interjecting an occasional two-finger duet with her great-grandchildren, Lord, and me, her oldest grandchild, she presented a recital, echoes of her fine music from days gone by reverberating between the notes played by now arthritic but still agile hands. We all applauded each other and played a jolly encore.

Without their youthful insistence and sturdy assistance, she would've been anchored by a broken hip to her room, Lord. Nonsense they said, carrying her along on their visions of what could be even past others' hesitations and desires to protect this now fragile ancestor.

Adventure, though, at the hands of great- and grandchildren was not new to her, Lord, for she'd already been on a wheelchair journey to a canyon's edge; hoisted in her wheelchair into an airplane via a baggage lift; and across the span of the country despite objections of the more "sensible" family members. Grandchildren, coast to coast, helped tend her, inviting her into their lives; grandchildren also, Lord, were learning how to age vigorously and with courage. A blessing for all.

Grandchildren, Lord, are seldom afraid to kiss the powdery cheeks of grandmothers; seldom reluctant to hug brittle shoulders and humped over necks, for they understand that they have a healing touch that can keep grandma young. It is a gift from you, Lord, knowing that lively generations are an investment in everyone's future.

Let Me Help

My daughter and son-in-law can thank me later, Lord, and I chuckle in glee as I overhear my granddaughter offering to "help" her mom and dad wash the supper dishes. For while babysitting today, I introduced her to the joy of soap bubbles, vegetable brushes, kitchen sink sprayers, and "helping" Mammaw do our lunch dishes while standing on a chair.

There was not a dry spot in sight.

She is as proud as punch, though, nodding her head and assuring her bemused parents now, "I do it. I help," remembering the pride she felt in a "clean" kitchen.

Blessing or curse? Lord, as parents, we often wondered which are the efforts of children learning to take care of their world. There is no doubt, however, that the efforts of grandchildren are blessings, for we grandmothers have the luxury of memory, recalling the generation we raised when their efforts seemed more interruption than assistance. We wish we'd recognized them as blessings just a bit better, Lord, for we still miss those fast-flying childhoods. So it is, now, Lord, purely joy to stand at a soap-splattered sink with a small child.

At a grandmother's knee is the best place for learning how to unload dishwashers and dryers, fold clothes and water flowers even to the point of water-logging the blooms, for there is no more important task than helping out.

Your patience with us, Lord, is so much like a grandmother's as you let us splash and play, get distracted and make messes while we, too, are learning how best to do it.

Stroller

It has taken me thirty years, Lord, to learn how to *stroll* a stroller, a lesson I'm mastering in the wake of a small grandchild who wants to go for a ride in her "Whee."

Before, I've pushed, pulled, hurried, propelled, raced pell-mell, aimed, and darted a stroller. Always in a hurry, always on my way somewhere other than where I was: in the present moment.

I regret, Lord, those rush-about days when I too often seemed to be waiting . . . waiting for another moment to happen, waiting for the children's bedtimes, their next growth stage, their independence; waiting for my independence, my bedtime, my next growth stage.

Waiting, Lord, waiting, for I was certain that the grass was greener at the end of the path I was hurriedly pushing the stroller down.

Now grandchildren have poked a stick in the spokes of my spinning wheels, Lord, showing me that to be content is to slow down enough to hear acorns fall, enough to catch "cotton" from my cottonwood trees, enough to smell the lily of the valley. That to take leisurely strolls is the proper speed for savoring. That grass underfoot is the lushest crop of joy as it unrolls beneath the wheels of a slowly spinning stroller. That strolling is the best pace for a walk in your world, a little child leading.

Perhaps, Lord, this is what I was in such a hurry to learn.

Sunrisers

The crack between first dawn and breakfast belongs to me and a visiting toddler granddaughter. Up too early because there's a lot to do and see at Mammaw and Bappaw's house, she settled for me so that her mom could go back to bed.

What an honor it is, Lord, to be the guide on dawnlit expeditions.

These are the times I most often missed when my children were little, and I am sure you recall my prayer-whispers from back then, Lord, *"Please, please, let them sleep just five more minutes."* I was so tired I frequently dozed through those too-early moments, sometimes, I confess, even feeling vaguely resentful at being pulled from my unfinished slumber.

What a loss on the one hand; on the other, what a joy it is to do it now with a grandchild. Yes, Lord, you can be certain, I am dropping a few gentle words in the ear of her tired mother: enjoy even the interruptions, for they are disguised invitations into this young life.

It is a good theory, Lord, for I, too, am so sleepy I have to remind myself to "enjoy." I'd only just gotten used to sleeping through the nights, having finally moved beyond the parenthesis of sleepless motherhood, colic to curfews. Now again, I am up too late at night and too early in the morning at a grandchild's beck and call.

Her little hand is soft tracing my face, Lord, in the pale dawn light, and I have tucked these tiny handprints into my soul to be retrieved and relived the next time I hear her too-early summons. I'm changing my prayer now, Lord, no longer praying for more sleep but instead for more sunrising moments.

Redbirds

When you think about it, Lord, no one should've been surprised when the elderly grandmother took him in. She, after all, had had a long lifetime to master the ways of loving. So, when AIDS struck her beloved grandson at the prime of his life, she simply made up the extra bed in the spare bedroom and brought him home.

It is a task calling many from retirement, Lord, as society . . . which simply means the rest of us, I confess . . . and some parents turn their backs on those stricken by this dreadful plague. Judgment, debate, fear, blame, shame, and conjecture flurry about, Lord, while grandchildren are dying.

In the midst of it, many of today's grandmothers and grandfathers have been endowed by you with special gifts—flexibility, tenderness, acceptance—Lord, and I am humbled by their use of them. They can transcend pubic opinion, grief, fear, gossip and aging's limitations to cut right to the heart of the matter: something needs to be done, I will do it.

Place your hand beneath theirs, Lord, steadying the faint palsy, straightening the arthritis, so that they can pour medicine, wash backs, and ladle soup into the sick and dying grandchildren. Those children know who to turn to when the world has shut them out.

Your love, sunlight warm and so bright it stings the eyes, is visible and strong, Lord, in the lives of these grandmas and grandpas holding today's vigils. Let the rest of us take note.

And like the caring redbirds who, if their young die, will even feed fish, bless the grandparents who continue to share and care long past the scheduled time they should.

"A" may stand for "AIDS" in this day and age, Lord, but it also stands for "Angels," grandmothers, grandfathers on call.

Road Maps

Always fond of starting projects that
have no end, I am making a patchwork
quilt for my granddaughter. Its beginning is
concocted from scraps of a season of
clothes I sewed for her first birthday. Over-
alls, lace-encrusted paisley dress and
bloomers, pinafore, wooly hooded cape.

The pieces, like a refolded roadmap, will
forever remind me of the cool early summer mornings I spent sewing its beginnings
on my screen porch. The bluebirds came
by, a papa wren flew over with news of
babies, and Mama Woodchuck and her
two lumbering toddlers came up from the
woods to sample my herb garden.

It is a beginning to savor.

Being honest, Lord, I think I am making
the quilt for myself so I can keep track of
where I've been with her, what I've done
alongside her, weaving all our many selves

into it, for we will never be the same as we were at any single moment, except as one of my patches.

I will stitch it together with fine threads of wisdom, a fancified word, Lord, which simply means lessons learned thanks to your redeeming power, because parents, grandparents, children, and grandchildren raise one another, snuggled together beneath a patchwork quilt of love.

Different Drum Beat

Deliver me from toys, Lord. Stacks, aisles, catalogues, and entire stores devoted to giving me a headache. And a heartache, for there is little to satisfy anybody for very long in any of them.

Plus, Lord of endless ideas, today's toys are making me lazy.

Why, for instance, should I make drums out of oatmeal boxes, cookie tins, and kettles when there are plastic ones ready for the taking? Why should I save thread spools to make necklaces when I can buy an already painted assorted set of them complete with string?

Cartoon sheets and commercialized games are simply gameboard-sized advertisements. Clothes, sandals, Bandaids, and toothbrushes all boast someone else's creativity, Lord, leaving us bemused and empty-handed if not soon to be empty-headed. We need to exercise our imaginations and, monkey- see-monkey-do, our grandchildren will think not only that milk comes from cartons, but also that play comes from plastic.

Fill our pockets and purses with handkerchiefs to make into dolls; scissors and paper for paper dolls; string for figure-making; yarn for finger crocheting; paper clips for necklaces; crayons for rainbows.

Deliver us, grandmother and grandchild, from toy store aisles, and send us instead, Lord, into the wells of imagination so that we can turn the ordinary into extraordinary.

These youngsters need to know more from us than how to shop.

Living by Degrees

I'm unsure whether this is a boast or an apology, Lord, but while many of her peers are getting Ph.D.s, my daughter is getting training pants and purple dinosaurs for her daughter.

She frets a little, worrying that life is passing her right by while she works at a job with flexibility rather than a future, while she memorizes "Baby Songs" and the "I Love You" purple dinosaur song rather than theories and methods. She is a wife, mother and stepmother, Lord, and it is not *what* she does that matters, I tell her, but *who* she is that gives meaning.

Yet these are tedious times, Lord, when our daughters are caught in the "correct-ness" crossfire: you are chastised equally whether you are a full-time stay-home mom; a full-time professional plus mom; or part-time professional and part-time mom.

All sides need to listen to a chorus of grandmothers, Lord, for we have bifocal vision into these matters, seeing both behind and ahead. Our message, sung as a descant to your directives about "putting lamps on hills, not beneath baskets" is that there is a calling for each one. Like all other bits and pieces of the mosaic of your creation, each one is good, very good.

Give this grandmother chorus, Lord, words and melody to share in verses about savoring today, applauding one another's choices, helping out, letting tomorrow take care of itself.

And remind us to sing a verse about the resiliency of children: they overcome most parental behavior. Send *our* children to the mirrors, Lord, to see in their own reflection, proof of just how wonderful children turn out, regardless of what their mothers, we, did during the day.

Help them learn to enjoy their choices, for this is the verse children most often repeat.

Round Trips

I learned a grandma lesson the hard way today, Lord: never take a grandbaby on walks farther away than a distance you can piggyback her home!

How many times, I wondered today as I huffed and puffed on the return trip, have you carried us all, Lord, for no matter our age, even we grandmas stray too far and have difficulty getting back home.

Our straying is not the same as the children/explorers, Lord; it is instead often passive and pathetic. We also even confess to a little mid-life short-sightedness, Lord, when we can only see over our shoulders behind us to places we have been.

And so we sit on our laurels, or we coast to a stop, certain we have nowhere else to go and no energy to return to the starting place for further instructions, information, inspiration: at your knee.

Yet, gifts from your hand, here come these grandchildren who want to see beyond corners and, in the exploring, kick the dust bunnies in our settled souls high in the air.

They whistle and beckon us to follow; they always want to go a little farther than they have stamina for . . . a perfect counterpoint to our hesitancy. They revitalize us *despite* us, for somewhere we discover we do indeed have the energy to make round-trip journeys together. We, too, want to see around corners.

Together, Lord, together we, old and young, can travel the distances you invite us to cover. Teach us to judge our own distances, Lord, from here to the corners where you wait. And when we get weary, grandma and grandchild, carry us both.

Rainbows

I never thought about the sisterhood to which I now belong, Lord, until I watched the news tonight. A shriveled, war-scarred grandmother looked straight through the camera at me, her starving grandchild in her arms, and I recognized the urgent message in her eyes: save the children.

It is a sisterhood, Lord, of Global Grandmothers.

No matter where we live, peacetime or war, starving or overfed, we all want the best for our grandchildren. In some cases, Lord, the best is simply to live until morning, and I weep at the thought. How can they bear to lose their precious grandchildren? How can they remain believers in peace, goodwill, hope, when there is none for their third generation?

Outdoors, as I watched the gruesome news, Lord, a thunderstorm was raging. Through the far window, however, I could see a rainbow unfurling itself in the sky, drawing me out in the aftermath of the storm.

It is no casual coincidence that you spread your rainbows, Lord of promise, over us all, stretching it like arms to include both the televised grandmothers and those of us who watch.

Now standing beneath its promise amidst the dripping trees, I lift my eyes to you, getting the message: tomorrow *can* be a better day, of peaceful beginnings to healing of ageless battles; tomorrow *can* be a stronger day of reclaiming neighborhoods and communities; tomorrow *can* be a cooking day when our grandchildren will all have enough to eat.

To make it be so, line up all the grandmothers, Lord, sea to sea, beneath your rainbow umbrella, and send us into the fray of warring, hating, terrorizing. We will do whatever it takes to save one another's grandchildren; come, go with us.

Grandma's Intuition

We were right most of the time, weren't we, Lord, when the children were young and we "read their eyes" to see how things were going? I remain grateful for "Mother's Intuition," surely one of your best gifts to us, Lord, for it led me to sit a bit longer beside the bed after prayers, to push a little harder at a stubborn silence.

And now "Grandma's Intuition" is even better, Lord, for it allows us to check out both generations at once: child and grandchild. It is a marvelous tool, Lord, and with it we can hear the underground tensions, see the smoldering tempers, sense the isolating fusses, and safely intervene as the generations clash and strain in the inevitable struggles of growth.

As with children, Lord, separating adversaries works best. And where better than Grandma's house? Have the grandchild overnight to make cookies; have the parent for lunch to catch up.

We can give someone a little extra pat on the back; a little extra support; sympathy; understanding; a sack of cookies to take home; a day without having to share; a day even strapping teenagers and successful adults can be a child again because someone "big" is in the kitchen.

And, if both come for supper, we can be neutral territory giving each a chance to see the other in new light, just as you so often do us all, Lord.

There's no need for us to try to *say* something wise, Lord; it's more *what* we do, Lord, when we feel the hair tickle along the back of our necks . . . Grandma's intuition says time for an invitation.

Locket

Lord of recent and ancient history, the young woman in the faded photograph in my antique locket is my great-grandmother. What I know of her is as faded as the sepia tones in which she is forever smiling. Yet, in the wonders of re-creating, my new grandbaby and I share her eyes.

I was going to use the locket, a family keepsake, to put the grandbaby's picture in. Surely she will never change, I think, watching her attempts to walk, to feed herself, to name us all, to ride her trike, to throw a ball, to climb a ladder.

Alas, Lord, the locket is not big enough in which to contain all I already know of this child.

We put first our children, then our grandchildren, in lockets, behind plastic in albums, on reels of VCR tape and into slide carousels, convinced that they'll never grow up.

When I was a long-ago tired mother of young children, Lord, that seemed like a prison sentence of forever picking up small toys and food from the floor and wiping, teaching, cleaning, folding, and balancing career and home. At other times, I know now, it was a gift of innocence to think they'd be forever underfoot, for in reality, we raise them to go away.

And so, as the spools of life wind from one reel to another, Lord, remind us to look closely, listen and chat daily, hug hourly, if only in our imaginations; spill these daydreams over into phone calls, letters, visits, for we grandmothers understand just how quickly childhood becomes a faded photograph in a shiny locket.

Color Outside Lines

With gold and silver sprinkles, Lord, a meteor shower from your wondrous hand is scheduled to scatter itself across tonight's midnight sky. And if I have my way, Lord, the grandchildren will be wrapped in a quilt on my lap watching.

We can all nap tomorrow, lullabied by the silent melodies composed in our sleepy midnight minds as we "oooooh" and "ahh-hhh" at these shooting stars, for surely they must spin and dance to music as they unhook from their staid and fixed orbits.

Thank you for sending these playful nightsky visitors, Lord, reminding us to all become as little children, coloring outside the lines of our daily orbits. Our grandchildren, too, remind us how, Lord, offering us grand pictures of grape-purple puppies, popsicle-orange trees and rainbow-striped skies to display on our refrigerators.

Seat us beside them, Lord, the original painter of rainbow skies, for a spell of finger painting, squishing reality right between our fingers in satisfying squiggles. Send us outdoors with them to "paint" fences and buildings with brushes dipped in buckets of water. Shinny us up with them into treehouses where we can look down on our lives and discover that they will be fuller when lifted, like balloons in a sunshine sky, above rigid scheduling and constructing "oughts" and "shoulds."

I'm promising the grandchildren, Lord, that I'll invite them to the next eclipse of the moon, meteor shower and comet trailing across our lives. There is order in your universe, just as there is in our lives; but once in a blue moon, we can make room for the extraordinary.

For, as these grandchildren remind me, Lord, the world might actually be a better place with a purple puppy to walk through it with you.

Bending Twigs and Time

My grandbaby naps at suppertime, Lord.
Or what I consider suppertime. But whereas
I was a traditional five o'clock suppertime
Mommy, my daughter is a suppertime work-
ing Mommy and eats supper late with Daddy
and Baby, a meal they value sharing.

It's been hard to get used to, Lord, and
at first I was dismayed and on the way
toward disapproving. But, thanks to a
quicksilver memory of cows mooing, I kept
my mouth shut.

Remember all those years, Lord, of rear-
ing a trio on a farm? I connected every
domestic, family act including suppertime
to the strict schedule needed by our dairy
cows. We ate after they ate and were
milked, only then holding hands in grace
for your bounty, for they had to eat pre-
cisely on time lest their milk flow slacken.

Today, my daughter and her family, like
many of their peers, write their own sched-

ules, dictated only by a desire to be together, Lord, no cows mooing in the background.

And it works. The baby is thriving, likewise the marriage, Lord, and the job as well, lived by what appears to be a skewed schedule with nary a cow in sight. Yet, perhaps, Lord of unfolding revelations, perhaps the truly skewed schedules are those lived by clocks that decree mealtimes, naptimes and togethertimes with scolding hands and no provision for the truly best gathering moments.

Forgive us when we miss the point, Lord, of clocks and schedules; of ritual and tradition; of order and planning. They are to serve us, not the other way around. As we shift and adjust to a different world of family and modern grandchildren, Lord, unwind the dictating clocks on our antiquated walls, releasing us into the present moments of today. We could be in danger of ticking our lives away in senseless habits.

Taffy Pull

Along with hazel eyes and an appreciation of shoe sales, Lord, I hope I have inherited my grandmother's patience. It is amazing I never knew she had patience until I became a grandmother myself and realized that it is of the utmost importance that I never let grandchildren feel they are a burden.

Which I was, Lord, which I was. As are all children with their curiosity and questions, their need for eternal tending and vigilance and their assumptions that they are the sun and I am the planets, revolving around them. Which I do, Lord, which I do.

And which my grandmother did without dropping a note in the music lessons she taught others or a smidgen of sugar in the holiday fruitcakes we baked or a dollop of molasses in the taffy we made almost every Friday night.

Where, Lord, did she get the energy and patience to pull taffy with me? To wait for the sugar mixture to reach hard ball stage; to wait for me to reach the drowsy stage? It was surely from her knowledge of seasons that she understood children grow up and away before the sweet sugar of childhood barely begins to boil. And I am grateful for your passing on that knowledge to me, O Lord of busy Friday nights, moments which sustain me even today.

For I am proud to announce that the most splendid creations that have ever graced my kitchen are gingerbread houses built by the deft hand of a grandson come to stay over. He makes each section of roof a different flavor; each chimney a deliciously unique spire to reach into the blessed Friday night chaos, an echo of patient pleasure begat a half-century ago by another grandmother in another kitchen.

Proper Maintenance

Doggone that grandmother down the street, Lord. She gave her grandchildren electric cars which they've proceeded to drive with annoying, jealousy-invoking delight past my house and visiting grandkids.

Instead of toy cars, however, they've got me. I don't do cars; I try to do maintenance instead.

Maintenance. We do it for our real cars, refrigerators, furnaces, even VCRs, yet we neglect it for our families, Lord.

We confess that we put off, stall, hedge and postpone daily moments, scripting our grandmothering with, *"This weekend I will, if, I really want to, but. In a minute, honey."*

We believe it won't matter because we will do or give—*fill in your own blank*—to compensate. For me, an electric car would be just such a bribe, just such a salve to my conscience, Lord, for not having taken time to do the small stuff.

It doesn't work to dump gifts on our grandkids at birthdays and Christmas, Lord, to make up for a year of daily oversight, no matter how noble our intentions to "make up for everything."

For what we are really doing, we must painfully acknowledge if we are to change, Lord, is making children responsible for telling us—through their response to laps full of our gifts—is that, *"Sure, Grandma, it's okay."*

I hear you say, O, Lord of infinite small loving gestures, to forget their words and, instead read their eyes, for there the true tale is told: it's not okay.

No, it's not okay, Lord, that we require our grandchildren to dispense forgiveness for our negotiable grandmothering, no matter why we do it: time demands, distance, our own uncared-for lives. Forgive us for bribing these worthy grandchildren to settle for so little of us.

Meddlers

I am still searching for an answer to my friend's question, Lord, as to how much she should say about her son and daughter-in-law's parenting methods. They are mean to the children—her grandchildren—she says. She's kissed the bruises and burns, Lord, soothed the sobs and gritted her teeth all the while, for what is a grandmother to do?

She knows she should pick up the telephone and call for protective services for the children, for next time it might not be only a bruise, heaven forbid. Law and Grandma forbid, too. Give her the courage to do it and give me words of comfort for her, a snitch out of love.

There is many a sleepless night, Lord, for other grandmothers who lie awake "choosing up sides" within themselves: their adult children versus grandchildren.

Say nothing, do nothing versus interfering
. . . which is how any comments are
labeled, Lord, even when meant only to
help.

Always the price is high, for the grandkids might be lost either way: if they are
being harmed, they withdraw even from
the grandparents. And if the parents take
offense, **they** will withdraw the children.

Isn't honesty, Lord, the best place to
start? *Never* giving a grandmotherly plati-
tude in the face of real danger, *"Oh, you
must understand,"* or *"He/she really loves you
. . . it's just a bad time."* Children lose
twice, Lord, if we merely put cosmetics
over bruised little bodies and spirits.

Help grandparents know that concern
for safety is not meddling; annoyance over
style and approach may well be. Be with
those who must decide—the sleepless
nights seem endless. May there be no endless nights for any of our grandchildren if
we can prevent it.

Second Chances

When he asks me to come see him pitch a baseball, sing a song, play a game, I go, dishtowel flying over my shoulder. When she asks me for a story, I sit right down, laundry left soaking, and let the "Once upon a time" magic take us wherever a tale leads.

Once upon a time, though, Lord, I was not so attentive to the small ones who shared my life. Once upon a time, I was not so patient, so laughing, so relaxed, so approachable, so quick to respond and share. Instead, I stalled, bargained and put off.

It would be great if I could redo those once-upon times, Lord, applying what I've learned through the mellowing years. But, thank heavens, it is not to be.

Yes, Lord, thank heavens, for at first I thought it could happen through the grandchildren and that I was being given second chances to do a better job. Yet, what a thief I would've been had I edged my way into a family portrait between parent and child.

What is done, is done, and we traveled by the light we had at the time, Lord. And while it might make us feel a tad better, Lord, grandchildren are *not* opportunities to improve what we did as parents. For, although we may have learned and could do a better job second time around, these children belong to their parents.

And besides, Lord, we are relishing the role of GRANDparent; with your re-creative presence beside us, there can be no grander a place to stand today than one generation removed.

Mixed Blessings

It is usually an act blended equally of both love and necessity, Lord, for those grandmothers who must raise their grandkids. They are everywhere: stores, malls, museums, parks, their own kitchens. You can see them, Lord, scurrying to keep up with small fry who are at least two jumps ahead.

More than just babysitters, Lord, these grandmas make the homes, the meals and memories for children whose parents are Elsewhere. And if that Elsewhere is a sad place, perhaps even divorce or death, a grandma is solace and security. The next best thing, Lord, a child can have.

Bless the efforts of these grandmothers who fill this void; give them energy and humor for the fulfilling of this unexpected chore just as they'd thought to be free. Help them retrieve at least a little of that freedom and independence, Lord, in between tasks.

And if it is a temporary situation which will send the grandkids back to perhaps a less than wonderful home, Lord, nurture the grandmotherly hopes that at least she has planted seeds of being loved . . . and being loveable . . . in young minds who must now leave her; that she has offered them options of living to surround them with love and support in all their days ahead in the new Elsewheres they face.

And, Lord, on the day when they do leave, hold her in your arms and cradle her as a grandmother does a lonely child; it is equally hard to see them go.

Thermometer

Fork poised between omelet and mouth at the restaurant, I watched the tall, cool dude of a teenager two tables away with his family shy from his mother's concern. How many times have you and I, Lord, heard that ringing accusation at *my* motherly concern: "I'm fine . . . leave me alone." Yet, I, too, even from a distance, thought he looked a little feverish.

Sure enough, by the second cup of tea, Lord, he was leaning against his grandmother's hand placed against his forehead. "Fever," she pronounced, calmly pulling a bottle from her purse and handing him a couple of aspirins. Gratefully he swallowed, nodded his thanks and momentarily laid his head on her shoulder.

Mothers may *know* things about their children, Lord; grandmothers can get away with *doing* something about it once they are "grown up."

Touch, sight, smell. Scientists reported not long ago that mothers in a study could identify their babies by smell. And we can read pain in their eyes as well, Lord, yet another gift from you which improves with age, just in time for teen grandchildren resisting that motherly bond. We are never more needed than now.

Thank you for this special spot from which we can tend grandchildren, Lord, little ones and big, who never outgrow their need for being cared for. Once it was tonsils and scraped knees that Grandma's kisses healed; today, it is faltering esteem and vanishing innocence which ails them.

We grandmothers can be counted on to have potions in our purses, cool hands for feverish brows, and shoulders for leaning. A safe distance from home and motherly concern, we are the first stop away; keep our aspirin bottles full.

Who's Handicapped?

Grandchildren are embarrassing, Lord, asking questions for which there are no answers, *and* in public. *"Grandma, why did God twist that man up so bad?"* I overheard children asking in voices that careened the length of the store aisle and back again. A chorus of turned heads, mine included from its spot behind the cereals, followed a small boy and girl's pointing fingers to a severely crippled young man propped into a gadget-laden wheelchair.

Why, indeed, Lord?

Stranded with not a very good answer between the frozen foods and dog food was neither the time nor the place to discuss the randomness of health, and I leaned to hear her answer. And where were you, Lord, who handles these complexities? Yet there the question was, as the children searched the young man's face for an answer, for surely he had wondered himself, "Why, God, why?"

You've heard it before, haven't you, Lord? For I suspected from the look on his mother's face, standing sentry-proud behind his chair, that this is a familiar question you and she ponder, and instinctively I felt a look of apology for having two whole, wholesome and rambunctious grandchildren and three whole, all-grown away children flatten my face into a grimace of guilt as I cowered behind the shelves.

Why, God? Why her, not me? Why is any child, grandchild, in your creation so contorted? Yet, even as I ask, I know that you didn't will this, and that you joined all of us that grocery shopping day.

For you were there, Lord, in the young man's words, *"It's okay to ask and look,"* he smiled to the children, adding, *"can you believe I am a champion wheelchair racer?"*

"Grandma, can we go watch him?" begged the questioners, their first query forgotten, the answer to it no longer needed. The

only answer to *this* question was an affirmative nod; the only course now, Lord, is for us all to become cheerleaders, led by children who remind us to look beyond the obvious questions.

Bless the grandmothers who help their children bear the daily efforts of their handicapped children; bless those who never give up on their special grandchildren; who never apologize and who show photos in billfolds and celebrate triumphs so small most might not notice. Bless their grandmotherly strength for all to lean upon.

And, Lord of spirit-filled winds, grant this young man an extra strong tailwind as he races, leading all of us on his rubber wheels toward acceptance, support. Or at least enough understanding to stay out of handicapped parking spots . . . and if our grandchildren should notice when we don't, remind us there is no answer to why we are so embarrassingly thoughtless.

Bamcerto in G Flat

It is a nocturne of love, Lord, that we are playing today. Transported over nearly a day's travel and down five generations, my grandmother's piano now rests in my daughter's home where its lid is kept open, its keyboard in easy reach of her toddling daughter and energetic stepson.

Composing a gentle duet of blended family, he and stepmother sit side by side on the bench where he learns to play songs she first learned; where he learns to trust his inclusion in this new family, for they are songs I, and my mother before that also played, and I hover nearby to turn the pages in dog-eared songbooks. Pupils and teachers, yet who, Lord, would venture a guess as to who's learning the most about being loved?

And today, Lord, if you listen closely, you can hear the unmistakable strains of a

"Bamcerto in G Flat," the name her grand-father, "Bappaw," has bestowed upon the wonderful music her tiny hands make. Lovingly she pats and gently bams the tin-kling high notes; delightedly, she growls in unison with the deep, bass notes.

At both ends of the scale, Lord of gener-ous invitations, both children feel wel-come and secure, for they are not told "No," or "Quit making all that noise."

We so often close the lid on opportuni-ties for our children and grandchildren to expand and explore, ignoring ways we can become, even in times of broken and re-blended families, connected to one another. It is always you, Lord, turning the pages.

So, remind us, Lord, to keep the lids open on our pianos, paint boxes, brief-cases, recipe files, since our openness strikes the first note for these exploring grandchildren in the musical key of "B curious."

Follow That Spot

Old-age brown spots, I've just discovered, Lord, punctuate my arms like a dot-to-dot puzzle. When did the first one appear? When did I begin mellowing, melding, moving into middle years? When did it get to be a chore to move, jump, climb, run, bend? When did I get to be so soft?

Grandchildren bring with them reflections in a mirror of the older woman I will become. The image is both an unexpected chill worry *and* unimagined ray of warm pride and joy like a sudden shaft of sun, for I have earned every grey hair, every jot of wisdom, every smile and wrinkle line. Every brown spot.

Yet it has suddenly occurred to me that if I want to walk through my own woods with them, and climb this summer's Scotland crags, I must get in shape, not get old. I must move, not mope about old age brown spots.

If I want to carry the little one in my backpack and follow the bigger one to the peaks he seeks, O Lord and builder of our vacation mountains, I need to strengthen my calf muscles; prod me to do it. Hold me erect, shoulders back against middle-age humps, so that she can sit atop my shoulders, clutching my hair like reins as I gallop toward adventure, not falter to a stop.

Walk with us on the treadmills, Lord, and as we pump and pedal bikes, discovering just how delightfully easy it is to trade laps of fat for laps of walking around tracks and neighborhoods. Around vacation hillsides.

Stretching and bending in the glorious flexibility you offer in a self-tending lifestyle, Lord, is an investment in a grandchild's traveling companion. Our brown spots are nothing more than points of interest on a map.